Read: [*v*] The act of interpreting and understanding language, symbols, and the written word.

Furiously: [*adv*] To do something with excitement and passion.

Read Often. Read Well.
Read Furiously

Introduction

Genealogy is, I find, endlessly fascinating. I have a reasonable amount of birth, baptism, marriage, and death dates, along with infrequently-used middle names, for generations of ancestors. That's objective information. However, what I'm interested in exploring is the subjective stuff: stories of experiences and adventures, pictures, treasured items, souvenirs, and, especially, places.

My quest came into focus as I researched and explored: I was interested in my mother's Brooklyn, where she lived until she was married and World War II was over. My human primary sources for this type of information are gone, so I had to explore places myself and study photos. Growing up, I paid close attention to my mother's stories of childhood and family, so those are also woven in. Occasionally, her stories helped me ferret out some truth—I think. That's key: this little book contains quite a bit of conjecture built upon the facts I know. The conjecture is the personal perspective, the subjective information, that hints at the personalities of two parents (when they were young and not yet parents) and six ancestors waiting to meet you in these pages.

The facts, observations, and revelations will not fit together like the pieces of a jigsaw puzzle, but they come together after multiple trips to Brooklyn to explore and research and to form a story. There will be gaps and pieces missing that I might not ever discover, but before my time is up on this planet, I wanted to put together what I have and what I could find.

So, let me tell you some stories…

BROOKLYN FAMILY ALBUM

The ground beneath my feet seemed revered, almost sacred. I knew little about Brooklyn, other than what my mother had told me, when I joined a photo tour destined to photograph the Brooklyn Bridge and Lower Manhattan. This was the mythic place where my mother's family lived for more than two generations, and although this tour group didn't see much of Brooklyn besides the bridge, the seed of inspiration was planted: I had to explore this borough of New York City.

"I'm walking on *Brooklyn* sidewalks!" was my thought as the six of us left the Brooklyn parking garage on a bright sunny day with our teacher, David Simchock. The concrete sidewalks and macadam looked the same as anywhere: my hometown, your hometown, your second cousin on your mama's side's hometown. Reader, put yourself in my walking shoes: these were BROOKLYN sidewalks! My ancestors could have walked here! Externally, I was focused on getting to know the amateur photographers I'd spend the day with, along with learning some new photography techniques. Did these photographers know how important Brooklyn was to me?

"I'm walking on the *Brooklyn Bridge!*" I scored some great photos of the bridge towers and cables, as well as some of the downtown Manhattan skyline reflecting the morning sun. My mother's family didn't mention the Brooklyn Bridge much, so my thrill here was based on the bridge's iconic, historical, and media-based status. This massive structure was designed and built by a couple of generations of Roeblings (John, Emily, and Washington) from Trenton, NJ, where they are still legendary. (I live near their old stomping grounds.) It was dangerous work (John R. didn't survive) and took fourteen years to complete.

I've been more than curious about Brooklyn since that photo tour. How did this city-within-a-city and its neighborhoods, diversity, and urban lifestyle shape my family? This is the region where my maternal ancestors landed when they came from Northern Ireland. It's where my mother and her siblings had their youthful adventures in the 1930s and 1940s, up to when the United States got involved in World War II and they were old enough to serve and start families. Could I get a sense of *their* city? What areas were important to my ancestors? Could I make any connections between old and new Brooklyn? What did my mother like to do before she was a married lady? What were my grandparents like before they became grandparents? Where did they go if they had free time? What were my great-grandparents like? Was Great-Grandfather Walker a coffee *taster* or a coffee *tester*? Having questions about one's ancestors is a universal human experience, right?

By age ten, my mother was out of grandparents. All of Mom's grandparents, and her parents, are buried in Brooklyn. My grandparents, mother, and sister were all born in Brooklyn and eventually left for New Jersey. Mom's parents lived there until retirement, when they moved to North Jersey. All four of Mom's grandparents were born in Ireland and came to New York, specifically Brooklyn, for roughly the second half of their lives. Are their hangouts and neighborhoods gone or can I access them, or the sense of them, somehow, now?

I drew this family tree to show people, andI always appreciate a tree in stories about families. In my tree, I love to look at the line of ladies' first names beginning with "M" going back to my great-grandmother (this same thing happens on my father's side).

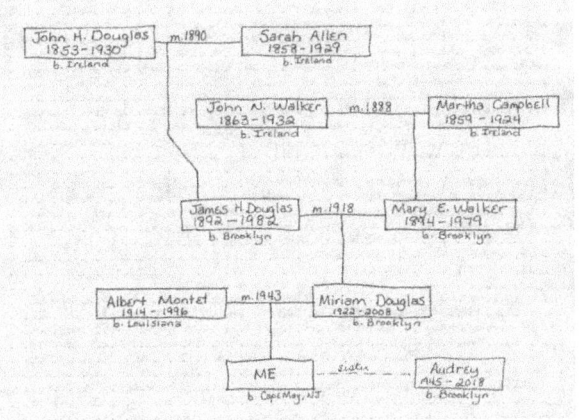

FAMILY STORIES

Memory is a funny thing. Two people, sisters perhaps, can experience the same event but remember it differently. My mother and her sisters remembered experiences in Brooklyn differently, and therefore recounted their stories to us children with variation. I know once my cousins read this book, some will confront me with details that don't match their mothers' stories. Does it matter? We creative nonfiction writers are encouraged to start tales from memory with a disclaimer such as, "The way I remember it..." So, for the stories that come from my mother's memory, please insert the phrase, "The way my mother remembered it to me..." if I have not already inserted such a disclaimer.

While we're inside our heads, let's consider dreams. In dreams, my mother and father appear middle-aged and healthy, the way they were in my young teen years. They are smart, productive members of society, frequently in touch with siblings and remaining parents. In dreams, there's not a hint of the dementia that would take my mother from me, and she's smart, gentle, and willing to nurture and spontaneously make French toast. She slips me twenty-dollar bills for gas money. In life she worried about me, but in dreams she doesn't seem to.

I miss talking about family history and secrets with my late sister, Audrey, and hearing her reminiscences of events before I was born. She, the oldest of our generation in our family, and I, the youngest, had different experiences. She was born at the Brooklyn Naval Yard just after World War II and remembered family get-togethers in that borough when everyone was young and there were fewer cousins. She remembered details of Chicago trips to visit with our father's folks when everyone there was younger, too. Unlike in Chicago, there are no strategically-placed cousins (that I know of) still in Brooklyn to visit and learn from.

With my family sources for anecdotal evidence gone, I've had to rely on two kinds of research: the pre- and post-COVID-19 boots-on-ground kind in which I travel by subway, taxi, automobile, and foot to inspect the sites, and the virtual research kind which included attending online tours, combing through digital archives and genealogical records, and reading books. I'll probably never find concrete answers to many of my questions, but my hope was to find out, as close as possible, what these ancestors' worlds were like.

Although I don't always adhere to a strict form when I write, like that of a poem or piece of classical music, I do like to have some kind of governing principle. As I learned more about this borough of New York City, I noticed that my story was unfolding in a kind of Joseph Campbell-style Hero's Journey, with me as the "hero" and the "journey" consisting of a combination of excursions and research. I imagined myself a twenty-first-century Luke Skywalker, Dorothy Gale, or Ulysses, classic heroes all, as I embarked upon this Hero's Journey, with the hope of emerging with the treasure of a sense of this place. Beware: heroes encounter barriers, too. Besides the unfamiliarity of the place, the COVID-19 lockdown and, after that, lung surgery delayed me from finishing my in-person research. Nevertheless, by connecting myself to scenes of Brooklyn, and connecting these scenes to my mother and her family, I learned about my ancestors.

"Brooklyn Heights, Bed-Stuy, Prospect Park, Bay Ridge, Green-Wood Cemetery, Coney Island—I will learn Brooklyn, I WILL learn Brooklyn," the hero repeated to herself. (I've added some information about the "Hero's Journey" trope in Appendix 1.)

Are you ready? Let's go to Brooklyn!

NAVIGATION

I knew I didn't want to drive to Brooklyn alone. I could get there in sixty to ninety minutes from my home, but what would I be able to see while wayfinding, navigating traffic, and looking for parking in what I understand to be a very busy city? That didn't sound like fun and I imagined myself hopelessly lost among Brooklyn-based ancestor-ghosts. The solution came to me after much rumination: why not think of Brooklyn, unfamiliar to me at the beginning of this quest, as an extension of the more familiar (to me) Manhattan? I've been going to New York City by train for years to attend concerts and visit museums. So, whenever I was unable to find an exploration partner for my Hero's Journey, I simply thought of Brooklyn excursions as day trips originating in Manhattan. I'd take a taxi or learn the subway to a specific Brooklyn destination, but was still a little nervous. In time, I chipped away at my *subwilderment*, a term I coined to describe unfamiliarity with the subway and thus hesitancy about taking this mode of transportation. A person gets turned around underground, disoriented when surfacing - even if they are heroes. As with any classic Hero's Journey, helpers and opportunities presented themselves.

THE BOOTS-ON-GROUND RESEARCH

A few years ago, alumni and current students from my MFA writing program attended a get-together at a September writers' conference in downtown Brooklyn. I was thrilled at the chance to become acquainted with this city-within-a-city. I could take the usual train to Manhattan and a subway to Brooklyn. Once settled in our hotel rooms for the weekend, my former classmates and I explored parts of Brooklyn together. On one of those evenings, Jessica, Abby, and I navigated ourselves to a spunky independent bookstore (Books Are Magic) on Smith Street upon Amy L.'s recommendation. After the bookstore, we met Amy L., Alison, Kerri, and some others for dinner at a large table at Bar Tabac, a few blocks away. Overall, it was a Brooklyn confidence-building evening inside a positive Brooklyn weekend experience. Later, during the COVID-19 quarantine, I'd be transported back to Smith Street when I read Jonathan Lethem's *Motherless Brooklyn*. The novel's characters did not shop at Books Are Magic or dine at Bar Tabac, but I felt a connection of familiarity when I looked up the novel's locations on my map.

JOHN N. WALKER

Unidentified, John and Mary Walker

I would later discover an ancestral connection to the neighborhood of my Brooklyn hotel. My mother's maternal grandfather, John N. Walker, the asthmatic one, lived about four blocks from my conference hotel at the time of his death! He died on my mother's tenth birthday, in 1932, so he wouldn't recognize much of the neighborhood now. ("Dude, where's my Brooklyn?" he'd probably say.) Next time I'm in that neighborhood, I'll be on the lookout for cornerstones dated before 1932 and imagine which buildings he would have known. Maybe I'll track down the last-known address listed on his death certificate, one of the few genealogical documents I have for this great-grandfather. I think of this kind of connection as a tie-in: there are two notions existing in the same place separated by almost one hundred years.

These two ideas are tied together in my head, but if truth be told, they only share geography and some buildings. The new experience only grazes the old one.

Campbell-Walker

I believe this is a family portrait. I don't recognize anyone, but there are names for a few of them on the back in faint pencil.

The people are grouped in a triangle: one man stands at the center back, then three men kneeling (I think), and four women sitting. The standing man is identified as Frank Campbell, my great-great-grandfather, or maybe a great-granduncle with the same name? He's smiling just a little and has his hand on the shoulder of the man kneeling in the center. All the men are wearing jackets and ties with white collars. All have mustaches. The middle man is wearing a vest and is definitely smiling. The man on the left is labeled as John Walker. He is not smiling and seems to be looking at something next to the photographer. He's my great-grandfather.

The prim ladies, all with hands in laps, none smiling, hair up, wear fitted bodices with many buttons. I wish I could see colors other than sepia. Lady #1 at the far left has two rows of bodice buttons in a V-shape. She has curly hair. She seems petite. Lady #2 might be called Katie, and has a small section of plaid-patterned skirt showing beneath her overskirt, which ends beneath her knees. One shoe is peeking out from under that plaid skirt. Her bodice is a solid color, smooth, with fifteen buttons, metallic I think, running up the center. The bodice has a stand-up collar with a bit of a ruffle at the upper edge. A pendant, possibly a locket, on a long chain, seems tangled in those buttons. Lady #4 is without a name. She has a similar high-neck bodice as Lady #2, but I count seventeen buttons on hers. She also wears a long pendant. Her skirt is made of tartan—a bold plaid. What are the colors? These are Scots-Irish people, so plaid is no surprise.

Lady #3 is my great-grandmother, Martha Campbell Walker. I can see my grandmother Mary in her face, but even more my mother, Miriam. The more I study her face, the more I see my mother there. It's eerie. I've only seen a few photos of this woman, and never noticed a resemblance. She's wearing a solid-color dress similar to Ladies #2 and #4, buttons blending into the fabric with a necklace, perhaps with multiple charms on it. One foot, her right, has completely emerged from under her skirt. Is that improper? Like her husband John, she's looking off to the side of the camera without seeming to focus.

The background is filmy—is it a sheer curtain with a window behind it? On the right side is a fireplace with shelves like a hutch instead of a mantel. There are things on the shelves - vases maybe - but they're hard to see.

Brooklyn Botanic Garden

My first all-subway excursion into Brooklyn occurred a few months after the writers' conference/reunion when Amy H. suggested we plan a road trip somewhere new. Amy is my niece, my sister's third child, a Jersey girl, and a social worker. She inherited my sister's love of travel and we occasionally set out on explorations, especially to locations likely to yield great photo ops. When she suggested we go somewhere in the spring after my sister died, the Brooklyn Botanic Garden was at the top of my wish list. I had been following the BBG on Instagram and wanted to explore the garden for its own sake, not for any genealogical connection. In fact, I don't remember my mother ever mentioning the place. Coming from opposite sides of New Jersey, Amy and I met on a New York-bound New Jersey Transit train on a bright April morning and flawlessly navigated our way by subway to the Brooklyn Botanic Garden. The Japanese cherry blossoms were magnificently blooming and the BBG was celebrating them. How lucky were we that we chose this April Saturday to explore? There were thousands of yellow daffodils on a hill, green palm trees in a humid building, and loads of other exhibits just waking up for spring. It took the better part of the day to explore the garden and have lunch in its restaurant. From one point in the garden, we could see a grand entrance to Prospect Park across the street. I explained to my niece that this is where her grandparents hung out when they dated during World War II. My mother's photo albums display many shots of each of them—my mother and my father—posing for photographs the other would keep close to heart while they were separated during the war. My mother talked about Prospect Park a lot. I wish I had listened more closely.

THE CHALLENGE TAKES SHAPE

A year after that first writers' conference/MFA reunion in downtown Brooklyn, there was another with a slightly different group of writers. For this long weekend, I challenged myself to function without the convenience of expensive taxis and entirely with public transportation, and I succeeded! I shared a room with Kerri this time. She had been enrolled in an evening creative nonfiction course I was honored to teach for my alma mater. She subsequently enrolled in the MFA program and attended many of the events for students and alumni. She was *all in*. In Brooklyn that September, we navigated to a professor's Gilded Age brownstone in the Bedford-Stuyvesant neighborhood with the help of Google Maps. This was brand new territory for both of us, but we found our destination with only a few hiccups in the pouring rain and wind, dodging abandoned broken umbrellas in flight. We were excited to catch up with our friends and mentors and peek at the inside of one of those mythic iconic brownstones. I didn't recall any ancestor connections to the Bed-Stuy area, but as Brooklyn goes, it's a happening place.

A month later, I found myself at another writers' conference, this time in the Chelsea section of Manhattan. This conference didn't suit me. *It's time to go*, I thought, as I considered my butt fatigue, the dark hotel basement where we all sat on hard wooden chairs, my difficulty hearing the speakers, and a certain particular New York City borough outside ripe for exploration—*it's time to GO*. I found an efficient subway line to Brooklyn and navigated my way to the Brooklyn Museum and the adjacent Prospect Park. (This had been my secret Plan B for the weekend all along.)

The Brooklyn Museum holds interesting treasures, including Judy Chicago's famous and transcendent *The Dinner Party* installation. I hadn't heard of it before I stumbled upon it that day, but I've seen frequent references to it since. Unfortunately, the museum did not have any focus on Brooklyn history as I had hoped. Although I had no anecdotal evidence that my mom had ever come here, it occurred to me while walking the rigid terrazzo floors that she must have. Maybe it's unlikely that the whole family of seven visited during the Great Depression when the kids were young, but could there have been a school trip? Did they do that then? Did she visit the museum with a pack of girlfriends or sisters? Sometimes we know the least about points of interest in our own hometowns, but I like to imagine that my mother was familiar with the museum.

I Google-mapped my way to Prospect Park from the museum. Specifically, I was headed to LeFrak Center. Here's why: for all of my life, my parents loved telling the story of how they met while ice-skating. They encouraged me to skate with friends at our county park even though I loathed skating. "Remember, that's how I met your father!" I went a few times, but I could never get the hang of it and spent my time leaning on the perimeter wall. I began to feel like my friends didn't want to go with me because I was such a lousy skater. In the end, I declared a moratorium on skating, and that was that.

The truth came out eventually: my mother didn't like skating, either. Her ankles wobbled and she fell down a lot. She also never liked the cold. Peer pressure was the sole reason she was at the rink that evening when she'd met my dad, a U.S. Coast Guard man from Chicago on liberty from his ship, possibly docked at the U.S. Coast Guard Training Center at

Manhattan Beach, near Coney Island.

I never gave much thought to where in Brooklyn this ice-skating might have taken place—some ice rink somewhere, perhaps Coney Island, probably long gone. They met in the 1940s, eighty-some years ago. But then, as I studied an online map of Prospect Park in my Chelsea hotel room the evening before my excursion, I noticed LeFrak Center. Could it be? Prospect Park was not far from my mother's family home in the Borough Park section, so why would she and her friends have gone someplace else further afield? My exploration of Prospect Park would focus on LeFrak then.

It was a long walk from the museum, but I had a mission. This was a viable link to an important location and event in family history and I was going there alone with Google Maps and a water bottle. I walked along the perimeter of the park so as to avoid getting lost in the twisting and winding trails, and spotted vintage-looking examples of landscape architecture that could have been placed there by park designer Frederick Law Olmstead and his partner, Calvert Vaux, themselves. (They designed Manhattan's Central Park, too.) Did my grandparents know this gazebo? Did my mother know that stone marker with the brass plaque on it?

Such Brooklyn day trips took on the aura of pilgrimages, especially when I knew a family member went to a particular place. I often had to remind myself to snap out of my reverie so as to take more photos and notes to study for clues later.

At Prospect Park that fall day, it seemed I had just missed a children's Halloween parade, and the costumed children with parents and bags o' loot were leaving through the various park access points. I doubt my mom and her sisters participated in anything like that. She had told me they dressed as hobos every year and begged neighbors for pennies and apples. Halloween then wasn't the holiday we know now.

My Hero's Journey to the skating center continued, something of an anticlimax once this hero's arrived at the skating center. Mid-century concrete-modern and full of promise for twenty-first-century skaters, but abandoned that day. I couldn't place my parents here in my mind's eye until at long last I turned around and noticed the lovely, natural Prospect Park Lake, in direct opposition to the concrete skating landscape. I felt a little tingly knowing that this *had* to be where my parents met eighty years ago! I had a visceral sense of the place. I decided that my parents and their friends would have skated on that lake in the 1940s rather than in circles on a rink. Yes, definitely on a lake. With this connection, my years-old mental picture of my parents skating at a rink similar to the one from my teen years merged with the new visual of Prospect Park Lake. It was the satisfying solution to a mystery.

I would learn from one of the many pandemic-era webinars I attended that people did, in fact, skate on that lake before LeFrak was constructed. Some functionary had the responsibility of measuring the depth of the ice, and when it was four inches thick, the area trolley cars would display a certain color flag as a signal that ice-skating was safe.

This was one of the many things I wanted to research at the Brooklyn Historical Society, which changed its name to the Center for Brooklyn History while we were all on lockdown. When the COVID-19 pandemic hit, that kind of trip went on hold. I wanted to learn more about skating at Prospect Park in the 1940s, where my grandfather's letter carrier route might have been, what kind of public transportation was available, and all about the Arbuckle Sugar

Company where my great-grandfather John N. Walker (the asthmatic one) worked, according to his 1932 death certificate, the census, and family lore. For the foreseeable future, though, my boots-on-ground research was halted, but I made do with books, webinars, searchable online library holdings, and interviews. Ulysses faced the sirens and the lotus-eaters, Dorothy encountered the Wicked Witch and flying monkeys, and I dealt with subwilderment and the COVID-19 quarantine.

THE 2 TRAIN TO THE CENTER OF BROOKLYN HISTORY

All through the COVID-19 quarantine, I was anxious to visit the Brooklyn Historical Society, as it was then called. I imagined naïvely that I would find the answers to all of my vague questions if I just went there and breathed the air. That was not to be.

Instead, I found most of my information slowly, tediously at times, through many scourings of their website and its links, my road and rail trips, and my reading of a pile of Brooklyn-themed books. When I started to emerge from lung surgery recovery (I'm fine, thanks), I thought about the Historical Society visit again, and discovered that the building at 128 Pierrepont Street was in the middle of a big renovation. I could visit, but I'd need an appointment, and to get an appointment I'd need to focus my queries. I also had to keep reminding myself that the Historical Society had a new name: The Center for Brooklyn History (CBH).

As it happened, my Brooklyn questions sharpened themselves as I chipped away at them throughout the pandemic and my surgery recovery. They boiled down to these three manageable queries:

1) My great grandfather's death certificate states that his job at the time of death was either a coffee *tester* or a coffee *taster*. Which one of these was an actual job title at Arbuckle Sugar?

2) Where would the closest business districts have been to my mother's family home? My grandfather delivered mail to one of these. Also, where would his post office have been for that area?

3) How would my mother and her sisters and friends, and their ancestors, have gotten to their favorite place, Coney Island? Streetcars (trolleys) or subways? Buses? Or a combination thereof?

There was a button on the CBH's website for an email-based virtual reference. As a librarian, I'm usually at the other end of those, and I felt obliged to do my own research. However, help might be the difference between finding answers and not, so I pressed the button. I typed in my questions, putting them in context, and in less than a week an archivist named Liza responded! Right off the bat, she solved the mystery of coffee taster versus coffee tester. I'll tell you about that in a moment. Which do *you* think it is?

The business districts and post office question would best be answered by looking at a land use map called *ZoLa* and some digitized directories. Liza sent me the links and I studied the contents carefully. There was actually a business district at the end of my family's street. I don't know if that was Grandpa's route, but it could have been, and the closest post office was a few blocks beyond. Considering the postman's unofficial motto, it would make sense to assign routes close to their homes:

> "Neither snow, nor rain, nor heat, nor gloom of night stays these couriers from the swift completion of their appointed rounds."

I know for sure Grandpa lived by this motto because my mother told me so. She recited it often to admonish me to take work seriously. (Parents should still do that.)

My public transportation question would take more work. Liza recommended a few books and atlases and invited me to make an appointment at the CBH. She would pull the materials ahead of my visit and then I could spend the afternoon reading about rapid transit in Brooklyn. Coincidentally, I'd be spending five days in Manhattan in June 2023, so I set up the CBH visit for the Tuesday of that week. I'd be visiting the New York Public Library, the Morgan Library and Museum, and now there'd be a third library on my itinerary. I amuse myself sometimes: after many months of lockdown and surgery recovery, where do I go? LIBRARIES!

From my favorite hotel in Chelsea, this was an easy commute: take the 2 train from Penn Station, ride seven stops, and detrain at Borough Hall in Brooklyn. This is the same downtown Brooklyn neighborhood I explored during those two writing conferences, so my subwilderment was at a minimum. I found the gorgeous terracotta-colored building in no time, and called the reference desk to announce myself as I had been instructed. At precisely 1:00 pm, an archives employee came to escort another researcher and myself to the third-floor library. I was finally there! Because of the renovation, I was expecting a plain, temporary room with a plastic table and uncomfortable plastic chairs. Ah, no. This library is magnificent: wood paneling, balustrades, tables, and chairs, a mezzanine level around the perimeter, brass lamps with white glass shades on almost every table, and a big, BIG reference desk from whence Liza appeared to greet us. We had been informed that we would have to check our bags and only use pencils for our notetaking. I had remembered that from Archives class in library school, so I brought a small notebook, a pouchful of pencils, my glasses, my excitement, and my phone to one of those stately tables. Liza met me there with my pile of books and a "cradle." This is a plastic contraption that holds (cradles) the book while the researcher reads in order to protect the binding. We are required to use the cradle.

My focus that afternoon was public transportation history in Brooklyn, but it was so easy to get distracted by my surroundings and photos in my books of subway construction in other boroughs. I reeled in my wandering eyes and imagination and learned that it really depended on where you started and your destination for which kind of transportation you'd use.

Starting in 1854, streetcars were powered by actual live horses. Some of the horse-drawn routes were replaced by steam trains as early as 1888, and in some places electric trains were introduced. When the horses were retired, tracks and overhead power sources had to be built to accommodate steam and electric power. Many of these lines were elevated. I remember my mom referring to "elevated trains," but I didn't know what those were until I lived in Philadelphia during college. Our "El" route was shaped like an "L" but was also elevated at either end. The trains went underground in the congested city, the part that I knew well.

In Brooklyn, subways started appearing after the turn of the century. Some of the cars were made of steel (heavy), some of wood (flammable), and some a combination. They were about fifty-one feet long and held fifty-two passengers. There was a "motor truck" at the front and the end of the train consist. Not all of the passenger cars came from the same manufacturer, because no one plant could handle the 500 cars ordered. Four companies built the modern new subway cars, and the first 200 completed were tested on the elevated railway.

All of that data is interesting, but what it means to me is that by the time my great-grandparents arrived from Northern Ireland, the horse-drawn streetcars had been replaced by steam or electric. My grandparents would have known about subways as children, even if they didn't yet have the opportunity to ride them. It took a long time to integrate subways into the rapid transit system because of a multitude of engineering hurdles: sewers, water and gas mains, telegraph and power conduits, surface trains, elevated trains, tall buildings, and building owners all had to be dealt with.

By the time my grandparents were adults and my mother and her siblings were children, the subway would have been viable transportation specifically for Coney Island outings. Until 1932, there were even open streetcars available to take people to the beaches. My folks could also have used a nearby subway line to get within blocks of Prospect Park, including three short blocks to the lake and ice-skating!

BREAK TIME!

Here's something that endures from my mother's youth that I enjoy today: chocolate egg creams. My aunts and uncles on my mother's side, all from Brooklyn, used to talk about egg creams. I thought a drink with an egg in it sounded gross, so I never pursued it. Then somewhere I heard that there is neither an egg nor cream in an egg cream, and that it's a completely delicious confection. They are on the menu at my favorite New York-style deli, Moish & Itzy's, the place I go before evening teaching or lecturing to load up on carbs for energy. My friend and I ordered chocolate egg creams one day and became hooked. My first impression was that the drink tasted like the liquid from an ice-cream soda after the ice cream had melted into the soda, but better. Egg creams are easy to make. I found lots of recipes on the web as well as recommendations for where to enjoy an authentic one.

Here's a recipe that combines the most salient attributes of what I found online:

CHOCOLATE EGG CREAM

3 Tbsp. Fox's U-Bet chocolate flavor syrup
¼ cup whole milk
Club soda or seltzer water

Put chocolate syrup and milk into a 16-oz glass and mix. Add club soda or seltzer slowly until the glass is almost full. All ingredients should be very cold.

It's important to note that there's some debate over whether the syrup and milk go in the glass first, or if the seltzer does. Various Brooklyn sources say syrup and milk first, so I'm going with that method. The recipes and my Brooklyn-raised coworker, Randi, insist that syrup must be Fox's U-Bet, which used to come in glass jars. Hard-core customers could get a pump to fit the jar, Randi told me (her family had one.) This is a delicious connection to family members of Brooklyn and one that I've preserved by concocting it at home!

ARBUCKLE, PART 1

The Arbuckle team: there's a check mark next to Great Grandpa's head

During the pandemic summer of 2020 and beyond, I attended frequent book talks, webinars, and virtual tours created and offered by the Boston Atheneum, the New York Adventure Club, public libraries, and other lifelong learning organizations. I became aware of new books I'd like to read and trips I would like to take. I learned about skating on Prospect Park Lake, some great Brooklyn Heights mansions, and the "Sugar Wars" of Brooklyn. My great-grandfather (the asthmatic one), John N. Walker, worked at Arbuckle, one of the two big sugar companies, as a coffee *taster* or coffee *tester*. As much as I enjoy flowery cursive, it can be hard to read accurately in an official document. Liza at the Center for Brooklyn History solved this mystery for me. Liza, archivist extraordinaire, found a mention in volume 31 of *The Tea and Coffee Trade Journal* from 1916 (now online) which said that coffee manufacturers had no other way to distinguish various grades of tea and coffee but to employ **coffee tasters**. (This is amusing to me because coffee is my kryptonite. I hate the smell, I hate coffee-flavored things, and in the one tricky social situation where I had to sip some to be polite, I felt queasy for days afterward.) That 1916 trade journal is even roughly contemporary with Great-Grandpa's employment at Arbuckle.

Back in early twentieth-century Brooklyn, John Arbuckle and his principal rival, Henry Havemeyer, manufactured both sugar and coffee and competed with each other. Both were located on the Brooklyn waterfront, where Arbuckle's building has now been repurposed as an office building just waiting for my future fact-finding foray.

GREEN-WOOD CEMETERY

Before my recent intensified interest in Brooklyn, the photo tour, and the events described here, I remember only two visits to Brooklyn. One was a random Coney Island trip when I was very little (more on this later). The other was for my grandmother's funeral in 1979 when I was sixteen and we followed the cortège from Northern New Jersey in our own cars. There was no navigation on our part, just following, and I remember little of that trip. Knowing my family as they were then, there was probably some quiet reflection and sharing of Grandma stories in the car. She was a strong woman who navigated her family through two world wars and the Great Depression, raised five kids, and crocheted an afghan for each of them, plus one for each of her fifteen grandchildren. She was a woman of her time, though, and never held a job, drove a car, or traveled by airplane. Now that she was gone, my grandfather was bereft, and she was to be buried in Green-Wood Cemetery in Brooklyn with her in-laws. Her parents are in Mount Olivet Cemetery, which is technically in Queens but right near Brooklyn.

Green-Wood is and was a hot property, the eternal home of many famous people, along with my maternal ancestors. (And no, I don't know why it has a hyphen.) It was designed to be a place of repose, but also a place of quiet reflection and restrained recreation. Visitors in non-pandemic times took trolley tours of the large sprawling cemetery. I learned from my book about Green-Wood that Leonard Bernstein is buried there, as are both Currier and Ives, as well as the Rev. Henry Ward Beecher, Jean-Michel Basquiat, and scores of others.

By the time Fred and I made our carefully-planned, socially-distanced trip to Green-Wood, restrictions had relaxed quite a bit. The Delta variant was threatening to put a damper on day trips, but for now we were free to roam about. We skipped the commuter train and rapid transit system and drove there, emerging from the car only to inspect the graves, creating a safe, contactless activity. We had masks. We had a cooler full of water. We didn't expect a lot of human interaction. We drove up on the New Jersey Turnpike, crossed the Goethals and Verrazano-Narrows bridges, and chugged through the grid of Brooklyn's streets and avenues to the gothic main gate of Green-Wood Cemetery.

Fred, by the way, is my domestic partner. "Boyfriend" skeeves me, but I have come to realize "boyfred" is a clever moniker. We've been together over fifteen years and often day-trip to unusual and quirky places by car: New Jersey lighthouses, the Roebling Museum, the Mercer Museum and Fonthill in Doylestown, the National Watch and Clock Museum near Lancaster, PA, World War II sites in Delaware, and now Green-Wood Cemetery.

We soon realized that the chances of finding the grandparents and famous people with the tools I brought were slim. My research yielded section and lot numbers, but the online maps we accessed had only street names. We doubled back to the grandiose gothic entrance gate because I had read there were maps and helpers there. A cemetery warden showed me their official paper map with section numbers labeled. He would be the only live human I'd encounter this day besides Fred. My grandparents' section would be easy to find in the far corner. I asked the nice warden for directions to Leonard Bernstein, who was not far from the gothic gate. "Go up Battle Avenue here, past the Revolutionary soldiers, and then park the car near the steps by Liberty Path. Walk along Liberty Path and you'll see he has a bench, but don't sit on the bench." I didn't, because it's a monument, made of the same kind of granite as the grave markers, and we are forbidden from sitting on monuments.

Leonard Bernstein is buried with his wife, Felicia, and his younger sister, Shirley Ann. Their markers are flat in the ground, not fancy at all, and the bench labeled "BERNSTEIN" is positioned behind the three markers among verdant plantings. It's a pleasant spot in the Green-Wood universe, but I had predicted that it would be grandiose, or that the grass around it would have been stomped down by visitors. People had been there, as many had left stones and someone had left a Tanglewood concert program, but it was not heavily trodden like I was expecting it to be. Starstruck with the maestro's remains under my feet, all I could think of to say was, "Thank you for the Clarinet Sonata." That piece, which relies on rhythmic prowess more than fiery finger-moving technique, saw me through some end-of-semester juries in college in which most other clarinetists possessed that coveted fiery technique. Parts of it anticipate his jazzy music for *West Side Story*, for which I should have also thanked him.

After our Bernstein visit, we skirted the cemetery on Border Avenue to get to Section 203, where my grandparents reside. Most of the stones with lot numbers are hidden now by overgrown grass and trees, so I had to walk the entire section systematically until I found them. For eternity, they are situated next to my grandfather's brother and his wife, each couple sharing a granite headstone decorated with etched flowers. I had been here that one time for Grandma's funeral, but when Grandpa died three years later, I had been far away at college and my mother said not to bother with the trip home. I was nineteen and listened to my mother, but I always regretted skipping his funeral. College was scary that freshman year and I didn't know what consequences would befall the bereaved. I told Grandpa's headstone that I was sorry I missed it and I thanked him for all of his hilarious stories. This first-generation Irish American was a master storyteller with a vivid imagination. I thanked Grandma for teaching me to crochet when I was a young teenager. Soon after that, dementia took hold and she stopped crocheting. I still do, though.

Fred was patient while I explored Section 203.

I never did find my great-grandparents, Grandpa's mom and dad, John H. Douglas and Sarah Allan Douglas. There was empty space where they could have been, but where were their headstones? That's a research project for another day. I saw familiar last names from my family tree, but the first names attached didn't match my direct ancestors. My family came to Brooklyn form Northern Ireland, so I wonder if Section 203 was a Northern-Irish community: the Orangemen of Green-Wood?

When I said I would be visiting Green-Wood, and mentioned that it was large (458 acres) and a *destination*, a friend asked if anyone famous is buried there. "Yes," I said, "Leonard Bernstein, Jean-Michel Basquiat, Currier *and* Ives, and Henry Ward Beecher." Since I had bragged about my grandparents' neighbors-in-perpetuity, I felt compelled to visit some of the more famous people. It's lovely driving around the cemetery on roads with names like Sassafras Avenue and Cypress Avenue. Mausoleums are mixed in with humble markers, fancy obelisks, rugged crosses, and even a modern mausoleum condominium. Finding their plots took the rest of our Green-Wood time. If we were going to beat rush-hour traffic in Brooklyn and on the New Jersey Turnpike, we'd have to leave after finding Henry Ward Beecher.

So ended our long-awaited visit to Green-Wood: lots of slow, patient driving, lots of walking on uneven ground, trees, more trees, angels, lambs, crosses, monuments, mausoleums, tributes, and finally an idea of what makes this cemetery legendary. I'll return to visit the Grands again, and maybe take one of the trolley tours or look closely at the assemblage of tree specimens. I've incorporated Green-Wood into my mental map of Brooklyn as a central and crucial location. The memory of sitting cross-legged on my grandparents' graves, just inside the noisy intersection of 37th Street and Fort Hamilton Boulevard, has joined their past with my present. This is the abutment kind of connection: my grandparents' plots under the large tree exist simultaneously with the noisy city culture outside the fence but have nothing to do with each other. Only the noise infiltrates the cemetery, and the rest of the realities simply butt up against each other at the fence.

GEEGAWS AND DUST-CATCHERS

Grandma used to tell her visiting grandchildren stories about the figurines and china pieces in her large dining-room hutch. There was a strange mustache mug (with a built-in shield to keep your Victorian or Edwardian mustache dry) and a cup whose pictures told a cautionary tale about a naughty little boy. My explorations and studies of Brooklyn caused me to consider some of Grandma's possessions that I had come to own, so while grounded during the pandemic, I looked around the house for Brooklyn mementos as prompts for conjecture-laden writing. I found a small, strangely-shaped pitcher which never got a Grandma story that I recall, so I made up my own description and imagined its provenance.

THE LITTLE WHITE PITCHER

You, with your bulging sides and delicate handle, have watched over my dining room for a few decades. Before that, you sat in Grandma's hutch, which was loaded with curious geegaws. She had a story for each, but I don't know yours. I imagine the other geegaws all found their way to other cousins' homes, but I don't know for sure. Not everyone likes little objects, dust-catchers, but I do.

Your shape is distinctive: rather than a round or cylindrical body, yours bulges out into three sections and each of these has three secondary bulges. I think of shamrocks. A green leaf decorates each center sub-bulge on your exterior. Each leaf is posed differently, but all three could come from the same plant. On either side of your front large section, under your spout, there is a narrow stripe of gold filigree with two pink roses. Between the other two sections, your dainty handle, with porcelain decoration of its own, is attached. The top of the white handle reaches inside, over your sculpted edging, which is smudged with the same green paint as your leaves. Your three sections narrow at about two-thirds of your height, creating a kind of waist. From your waist, the edging forms an upside-down peplum.

I want to know about your provenance. Did Grandma

acquire you new? Were you a souvenir of someplace? She didn't travel much since her young adulthood was concerned with World War I, bearing children, the Great Depression, and World War II. Did Grandpa bring you home from somewhere when he was a sailor in World War I? Maybe you were a gift from her sister Maddie, a Sunday school classmate, or a child. Did one of my great-grandmothers, Sarah or Martha, pass you down to Grandma? Did you perform some service for Mary, Martha, or Sarah's dining-room table other than just looking pretty? If so, you would have even more stories to tell me. Did there used to be a sugar bowl to match you?

You have no maker's marks on your bottom. Some other porcelain pieces in my hutch say "JAPAN" underneath, no doubt created and acquired before the United States was at war with Japan in World War II. You could be from Northern Ireland or Scotland if you belonged to a great-grandmother, or Woolworth's in Brooklyn if Grandma was your original owner. Your decorations reveal no clues that I recognize: leaves, pink roses, gold filigree.

After mine, whose dining room will you grace?

"Did you try a Google Images search?" Fred asked. I hadn't, so I took your photo and sent it into cyberspace, not expecting an exact match. Google returned just that: your twin, listed at an ecommerce antique shop in New York or

New Jersey. (They are vague about location.) Your twin was marked "sold out" but would have once been available for $38. Unfortunately, the seller didn't know any more about your twin than I know about you. She referred to your twin as a "creamer" and listed her measurements as 3" x 3" x 3". That's a match. What's her provenance, I wonder. Were you both purchased at the same store in Brooklyn?

GRANDMA

Her legal name was Mary Elizabeth (Walker) Douglas, and she would make sure you knew she was a Mary Elizabeth and not a Mary Ann. She was a no-nonsense kind of grandma who never wore anything other than a cotton housedress with an apron at home or a nicer frock for shopping or visiting. Either was worn with black tie-up shoes with a chunky heel.

When I appeared on the scene, all of my surviving grandparents were in their seventies, and all would pass away when I was in my teens. My clearest memory of Grandma Douglas is her teaching me to crochet. We sat on the living room couch at my house while she taught me the chain stitch and the double-crochet stitch needed to make granny squares. She only had to show me once and I remembered, and I made many more squares from scraps of yarn we had around the house. I built upon those basic stitches as I taught myself more crocheting techniques. Grandma made doilies and dresser scarves, usually white cotton, and lots of afghans. Every one of her five children and fifteen grandchildren had an afghan from her hook. My mother took hers to the nursing home with her, and I'm reasonably sure it was the last thing she recognized as her own once the dementia took over.

Grandma Douglas had dementia too. She died when I was sixteen and wasn't herself for years before that. Any other memories I have of her were from my childhood. She told me stories, many from the Brooklyn days, and showed me how arthritis bent her fingers. When she meant to point south at the window, her rogue index finger would point east at Grandpa.

Mary Walker (Douglas)

I have photos of a younger Grandma, one where she is standing on the Coney Island beach, and her extremely long, wavy hair is blowing in the breeze around her. It's remarkable to my eyes because I only knew her with white hair pinned up with black bobby pins, as older ladies did.

A much later photograph, from the 1950s, shows my grandmother and my teenage sister sitting in lawn chairs outside our house. My sister is holding a magazine and giving the photographer (our father) the hairy eyeball. Grandma is, of course, crocheting with thin white cotton thread. (Doilies are more portable projects than afghans.)

GRANDPA

James H. Douglas

A grisly movie about World War I got me thinking about my grandfather, James H. Douglas. The army movie with its soldiers caked in mud did not show his reality because he was in the U.S. Navy. For at least part of the time, he was stationed at the Brooklyn Navy Yard, possibly distributing uniforms and supplies. (Did someone tell me that was so?) We have pictures of him looking like a teenager dressing up for a masquerade. He wasn't, of course; he was an authentic sailor serving his country from 1918 to

1921.

Also in 1918, he married Mary E. Walker (aka Grandma). They had five children, of which my mother was the middle child. All five were raised in Brooklyn, and when those five began adulting and starting their own families, James and Mary picked up and moved to a tiny house in Northern New Jersey and joined social clubs for older adults. (My favorite club name was XYZ, which stood for "Extra Years of Zest.") I didn't know them until they were well into these retirement years. Their move to New Jersey ended Brooklyn's reign as our family's headquarters.

I have a fun souvenir from Grandpa: a purple bag from a bottle of Crown Royal whisky. This was a strange gift for a teenage girl, but it has held my various small clarinet accessories that don't fit in the instrument's case since high school. No one has ever asked this teetotaler why she had such a bag, but I'm sure it prompted some music majors in my orbit to wonder.

My mother always told me when the topic of the Great Depression came up (usually while watching *The Waltons*) that the Douglases didn't fare too badly. Grandpa was a letter carrier so he always had a secure government job, and on top of that, he was lucky enough to have had a route through a business district. Looking at old maps on the Center for Brooklyn History's website, I determined there was one such district at the end of their street: Fifth Avenue from 47th to 57th Streets. I remember Mom telling me there was a multiple-bay commercial garage at the end of their street. Could this have been his route? The merchants knew he had five kids and would send things home with him: my mother remembered toys and DOLLS (her favorite thing), but there was probably food, too. As a letter carrier he would also get to use undeliverable Broadway show tickets that bounced back to the post office. He would take Grandma on a date night or send his kids off in pairs once they were old enough to navigate the elevated trains, subways, and trolleys. These fond memories of Broadway were strong enough to break through my mother's dementia many years later. She didn't remember what shows she saw, but a PBS documentary inspired some rare moments of lucidity in her nursing home room. What would Grandpa have thought of that?

Grandpa was always a very social person and

loved to talk and tell stories. He had friends, possibly from the neighborhood, the Orangemen's Lodge, or the post office. The manly thing to do with the cronies was to head over to Sheepshead Bay, near Coney Island, for clam chowder. I don't remember hearing if he took Grandma, but he had a Brooklyn friend named Sloan that he still talked about in those retirement years. The famous and enormous Lundy's Restaurant started as a clam shack on a dock in 1934 and grew to be a landmark that served 2,800 customers at a time. Did Douglas, Sloan, and friends go there for chowder? Lundy's closed in the 1960s and is now subdivided into multiple businesses. My friend Sue and I drove through Sheepshead Bay on our way home from Coney Island, and it seems to be a lovely residential seaside community. We didn't see the old Lundy's building, though.

The poet Walt Whitman recommended the Sheepshead Bay/Coney Island area in 1847, before my great-grandparents landed in New York. He was a native of Long Island and was the editor of the *Brooklyn Eagle*, in which he placed an entertaining essay about a clam bake in Sheepshead Bay (or close by).

Half-past five o'clock had now arrived, and the booming of the dinner bell produced a sensible effect on 'the party,' who ranged themselves at table without the necessity of a second invitation. As the expectation had only been for a 'clam-bake,' there was some surprise evinced at seeing a regularly laid dinner, in handsome style, too, with all the et-ceteras. But as an adjunct—by some made the principle thing—in due time, on came the roasted clams, well-roasted indeed! in the old Indian style, in beds, covered with brush and chips, and thus cooked in their own broth. When hunger was appeased with these savory and wholesome viands, the champagne (and good stuff it was!) began to circulate—and divers gentlemen made speeches, introductory to, and responsive at, toasts.

-Walt Whitman, "Clam-Bake at Coney Island,"
Brooklyn Eagle, July 15, 1847

CONEY ISLAND

Miriam Douglas (Montet)

Coney Island was my most anticipated boots-on-ground fact-finding mission. Mom talked about seaside Coney Island all the time. I imagine it as her version of my Wildwood, NJ: a honky-tonk boardwalk with amusements, rides, and delicious, unhealthy snacks next to the beach. I suspect that Coney Island is the origin of this kind of casual entertainment. Atlantic City is a contender, but since Coney Island-style hot dogs are known in other places as coneys, I think the New York seaside location was the beginning. Coney Island was no doubt more charming in the 1930s and 1940s than more recent Wildwood or even Coney Island now.

With her fair skin, my mother wasn't much for

the beach, although I've located a great photo of her on a beach blanket at the Coney Island beach, in a bathing suit, applying lipstick. She has that curly, frizzy hair I inherited, longer than I'd ever seen it. She must be about twenty. She and her friends would have spent their time at amusement parks with names like Steeplechase, Dreamland, and Luna Park enjoying the rides and entertainments. Mom probably was remembering these Coney Island days when she and my father took me to the Wildwood Boardwalk. He would ride the wooden roller coaster with me; she preferred the log flume. Did Coney Island have a log flume? I wish I had thought to ask, but this turned out to be an easily-answered research question: it did!

Besides Green-Wood Cemetery, the other Brooklyn excursion I remember from childhood was a much happier one from 1971 or earlier when my sister and brother-in-law took my mother and me to Coney Island. My brother-in-law and I (as of spring 2023, the only survivors of the trip) don't remember a reason for that trip, but it must have been just a visit so that my mom could see the playground of her first twenty years. This was the place where she and her friends and sisters would hang out. There are many photographs from that time leading up to World War II, of friends, sisters, parents, grandparents, and unidentifiables enjoying the beach and boardwalk. Through the scrim of more than half a century, I don't remember much from this trip. It was just the four of us, as my sister hadn't had any kids yet, so I would have been eight or younger.

I remember not being terribly impressed. It looked like Wildwood, NJ, to my eyes. Somehow, it was simultaneously unfamiliar and strange. It's very likely that my sister and I went on a famous roller coaster that day. I was already a roller coaster aficionado at that age, having Wildwood so close. That Coney Island was an important part of Mom's childhood would not have impressed me then. Today I would give anything to hear her describe the place to me (Steeplechase and Luna Parks especially), the fun times she had there, and how she got there (subway, bus, or streetcar?).

I know Mom went to Steeplechase Park, which was established way back in 1897. From my twenty-first-century research, this seems to have been the big-name, popular destination. There were carousel-sized horses attached to a curved metal track, and full-sized people would sit upon the horses for mock races. Pictures I've seen show people having the time of their lives astride these horses. George Tilyou was the Coney Island impresario who borrowed the idea for this attraction from England. The horses were made of wood and, later, metal, and moved up and down as they went along that curved track, creating the illusion for the riders that they were taking part in a real horse race. Live horse races were one of the most popular spectator sports of the time. In reality, the wood or metal horses never left Tilyou's fenced-in fifteen-acre park for the duration of the ride.

Before he created Steeplechase Park, George Tilyou had already erected an early Ferris wheel, 125 feet in diameter, half the size of one he had seen on his honeymoon trip to the Chicago World's Columbian Exposition in 1893. That one had thirty-six cars which held sixty passengers each. Tilyou's wheel had twelve cars which held eighteen passengers each. Ferris wheels would have been old news for my mother's generation, and maybe even her parents', but is there any chance my great-grandfathers rode it? Were they daredevil enough in 1894? There is no record of this to be found in family documents. They would have been thirty-four (John N. Walker) and forty-one (J.H. Douglas) when Tilyou's Ferris wheel opened, and it's fun to imagine them taking a break from their menial coffee-taster and clerk jobs for a bit of a thrill. I don't know this for sure, but I have a hunch that Tilyou's Ferris wheel would have been too risqué for the ladies.

The hundred-year-old Wonder Wheel, another famous Ferris wheel, still spins and still shows up in popular media. The Wonder Wheel played a key part in an early episode of *Law & Order: Organized Crime*, and I'm talking pivotal scenes with fictional murder victims. There's also a movie (called *Wonder Wheel*) starring Kate Winslet where no one rides it, but the wheel is almost always in the background. Even in the characters' apartment, we see the Wonder Wheel spinning outside the windows. The 1950s of *Wonder Wheel* is later than my family's Coney Island experience, but the movie gives a good picture of the wheel, and of both the traditional carriages and the "eccentric" carriages that slide across the wheel's radius as it turns. These sliding carriages gave this kind of wheel the name "eccentric wheel."

The characters in the movie ignore all of the rides

unless they operate them. Kate Winslet's husband, Humpty, played by Jim Belushi, operates the carousel, so scenes happen there. Otherwise, the rides are in the background both literally and figuratively, just the same as when I worked in the cinema ticket booth one summer in Wildwood. My colleagues, college-aged or younger, might have used popular rides as landmarks or meeting spots, but ignored them otherwise. For fun with friends or dates, they'd go to restaurants, movies, or the beach, but rides seemed to be for kids and tourists. Similarly, the Boardwalk was for them a thoroughfare rather than a destination. *Don't walk the sidewalks when traveling north or south; they are narrow, sometimes dark, and you'll have to cross multiple perpendicular streets. Instead, take the "boards" to your cross street and cut over then.* The characters in the movie tended to do the same thing.

My mother never mentioned the Wonder Wheel or carousel, but I assume she rode both. I know for a fact that she did ride the white wooden Cyclone roller coaster, which also made a few cameos in the movie *Wonder Wheel*. The Cyclone, which dates back to 1927, has a 2,640-foot track and reaches a top speed of sixty miles per hour. It's a New York City

Landmark and on the National Register of Historic Places. The Parachute Jump, starting in 1941, pulled pairs of passengers under parachutes attached to one of twelve arms coming out of a 250-foot steel central tower to the top of that tower. Inch by inch as they ascended, the suspense grew until suddenly the 'chutes with people underneath were dropped for a slow descent. Mom was terrified of this ride but did it anyway. The Parachute Jump is the only part of Steeplechase Park that survives. Although it has lights to commemorate special occasions, it has not been used as a ride since 1964. Nevertheless, it too is on the National Register of Historic Places, a New York City Landmark, and an icon of Coney Island. Sue and I used it to navigate back to the car when our Coney explorations were finished.

My long-awaited Coney Island trip finally happened on May 13, 2023. I invited my friend Sue, another Jersey girl, experienced with Jersey Shore amusements, to accompany me. We met in graduate school for Library Science, and we've explored Madrid, Granada, Paris, and Manhattan together. Now we were going to take in Coney Island.

We drove north on the New Jersey Turnpike,

crossed two large bridges, touched Staten Island, and rode the Belt, Shore, and Ocean Parkways to Coney Island. The amusement area impressed my adult eyes as gaudy and not glamorous at all, but charming and uniquely historical all the same. The most famous rides on my to-see list were the Wonder Wheel (1920) and the Cyclone (1927). Both have existed since before or during my mother's childhood and my grandparents' young adulthoods, so I surmise that they rode on each, along with thousands of other Brooklynites. Sue and I dined at Nathan's as they would have, eating our hot dogs (okay, "coneys") on a bench in the sea air.

The Wonder Wheel was a pleasant experience: no stress and no Cyclonic terror (just wait—I'll get to that). I read about these historic rides before Sue and I visited, so I was aware that the red and blue cars swing and roll on tracks toward the center while the white cars along the perimeter stay stationary. We were in a blue car, reassured that we were enclosed, as if in a cage. Even knowing we were in an eccentric car, Sue and I were nevertheless both startled when our car reached the sweet spot where gravity took over and the car abruptly cascaded toward the wheel's hub. As the wheel turned, the car changed course and slid toward the circumference. It didn't matter that I read about this amusement's hijinks pre-trip, looked at videos, and explained to Sue what would happen: squeals of surprise and delight came out of our faces when our blue cage started moving.

After our two eccentric wheel revolutions, we circled on foot back to the entrance to read up on some Wonder Wheel trivia. The steel girders (painted green) were forged of Bethlehem Steel right on Coney Island beach! The wheel is 150 feet tall and was the tallest ride in Coney Island until the 250-foot Parachute Jump was built.

Now take a deep breath and hold on tight, for here comes the Cyclone!

In order to get into the car, I had to stand on the Cyclone's red leather seat, as everyone else did, and then insert my feet, one by one, into the very narrow slot in between my seat and the cushioned panel attached to the back of the seat in front. I couldn't see the floor. What were we getting ourselves into?

My knees dug into that cushioned panel. My extra-short legs fit into the space provided, just barely, but what do tall people do? Sue has about five inches on me, and I noticed her legs were slanted, not parallel to the track as mine were. She wasn't entirely comfortable, to say the least. The good news was that there was no way we would fly out of that roller coaster car. When the attendant put the lap bar down, we were even more securely stuck in there.

The car consisted of two sections, with four double seats in each. Fourteen other persons went on this journey with us. It sounded like any other wooden roller coaster as we climbed the first (and tallest) hill: a bit rickety and as if we were being winched up notch by notch. (We were.) Even though I knew my commitment had been made, I blurted out, as I often do, "I've changed my mind!" We summited, and then that old wagon took off at speeds approaching sixty miles per hour on the downhills, whipping around the tight 180-degree curves, ascending, descending, passing under wooden supports I was sure would decapitate me, and then after 2,640 feet of track, into a dark tunnel, and…stop. The ride was about two minutes, but I had to look that up because I had no idea. It's all a blur to me now because it was all a blur to me then. With my head like scrambled eggs or freshly mixed paint, I attempted to extricate myself from that seat. It wasn't easy without a strongman or crane to help.

On the way to the boardwalk bench that would be our recovery location for the next half hour, Sue said, "I'm surprised my femurs didn't snap!" Knowing I would have to eventually write about the experience, my reaction, at least on record, was, "I have no words."

Eventually, we found our way to a few gift shops where I bought a Wonder Wheel T-shirt to commemorate that delightful ride and a miniature battery-operated Zoltar fortune teller like the full-sized, coin-operated one near the Wonder Wheel's entrance. Did Zoltar ever predict my mother's or ancestors' futures? He's old enough.

PHOTOGRAPHS

I have a photo of my grandmother, her sister, and another woman sitting in a photographer's fake car from a generation before my mother's putting-on-lipstick-at-the-beach shot. In the photo, young Grandma sat behind the steering wheel of the photographer's phony car with Aunt Mattie and a friend in the raised back seat. This is silly because in her seventy-eight years on earth, Grandma never drove a car. The picture is labeled on the back retroactively in my mother's handwriting, "Mary Walker, Martha

Walker, May Johnson (friend of Mary), Coney Island" with no date. The use of their maiden name Walker would imply that my grandmother (Mary) and her sister were not married yet, but one day while studying this photo, I noticed the car's license plate: 41322NY. I realized the license plate number was probably a date. My grandmother, seated in the driver's seat, looks to be in her twenties. If this was April 22, 1922, as I think the license plate indicates, she would have been seven months pregnant with my mother! This is conjecture, of course, but I know what I want to believe. I find it hard to take my eyes off this photo whenever I encounter it.

If my guess about the date is correct, Mary Walker would be married with the name Mary Douglas, and this would be her third pregnancy. I really love old photos. Unfortunately, the Grandma-behind-the-wheel photo has gone missing. I've shared another Coney Island gem, though, which features ten young ladies in their white summer dresses and hats in a goat cart. Grandma is in the back row, far left.

IMAGINATIVE SCRAPBOOK

I collected fifteen photographs that had belonged to my maternal grandparents and they ended up in a box on my mother's porch. These are the kind of sepia portraits that are mounted on stiff cardboard. I imagine the portraits were taken for folks to hand out to friends and family in the nineteenth and early twentieth centuries. I put these fifteen unidentified people in a scrapbook.

The photos are morose, like unidentified orphans, showing people with dark-colored clothing and somber expressions (no teeth showing anywhere!). As I studied the likenesses, most from Brooklyn or Manhattan studios according to photographers' marks, but some from Iowa, Connecticut, Belfast, and Scotland, the clothing styles told me that these are not my grandparents' contemporaries, but those of *their* parents or grandparents. The clothes have a Victorian or Edwardian appearance. The ladies have bustles. Making a connection to these distant relatives from Brooklyn and beyond is not likely, but this collection of unknowns, curated now with twenty-first-century acid-free sparkly-printed scrapbook paper, is great for imagining.

Fiction to Set the Scene

While researching another recent project, I discovered that novels can serve as research tools. I wouldn't let my students use fiction for the kind of research they are required to do, but to get an idea of an author's perception of a place, some fiction is effective. (Turn to Appendix 2 for a list of novels set in Brooklyn.) While researching Brooklyn, I read *A Tree Grows in Brooklyn* (Betty Smith), *Motherless Brooklyn* (Jonathan Lethem), *Snow in August* (Pete Hamill), *Manhattan Beach* (Jennifer Egan), *Pineapple Street* (Jenny Jackson), and *Deacon King Kong* (James McBride). The Lethem and McBride books gave me a vague angle on a more modern, seedy Brooklyn. I enjoyed the colorful characters, but didn't learn much specifically about the place. These stories are for ambiance. I checked my map whenever the stories gave me street names or neighborhoods to gain some context.

I mentioned earlier that some of *Motherless Brooklyn* takes place near Books Are Magic and Bar Tabac. This is a tenuous superficial connection, but it was still slightly thrilling for me as I put together my mental map of the borough while sitting in a New

Jersey suburb. The protagonists in *Motherless Brooklyn* never dined at Bar Tabac, but some of Jenny Jackson's Brooklyn Heights socialites from *Pineapple Street* did. Jackson's contemporary characters also attended a benefit at the Brooklyn Museum. *Manhattan Beach* (Jennifer Egan) features many scenes at the Brooklyn Navy Yard, which was vital and historic for several of my family members. Pete Hamill's book, *Snow in August,* supplied a mid-century child's point-of-view, where characters were perceived as either heroes (such as the Brooklyn Dodgers) or villains (the Philadelphia Phillies).

Betty Smith's *A Tree Grows in Brooklyn* is another story, literally. It transported me to 1910s/1920s Brooklyn, specifically the Williamsburg neighborhood. The realistic fictional events took place only a few years before my mother arrived on the Brooklyn scene. These would be the years of my grandparents as young marrieds. Writing about the early twentieth century, Smith has impressions, fresh observations, and current slang in her writer's toolbox. I can picture my grandfather standing in an alley next to a bonfire with his cronies eating *mickies*: potatoes roasted in the fire. *Twenty-three skidoo* is an idiom meaning a hasty departure. It sounds like grandparent slang to me.

The child protagonist, Francie Nolan, tells the reader that the ailanthus tree is the "only tree that grew out of cement." This intrigued me enough to look it up. Should I plant a literary garden featuring an ailanthus tree? Nope. It's considered an invasive species and I'd *never* get rid of it.

I loved reading *A Tree Grows in Brooklyn*, but I didn't get around to it until after I passed my own half-century mark. I wonder why my mother never put this book in front of me. It deals with some tough-life topics like alcoholism, but so did other books and television when I was growing up. Did she not want me to have a picture of poor Williamsburg society because it differed from her own working-class childhood in Borough Park? Was she xenophobic about this? Why didn't I ask her? Why did my sister never suggest it? They were both avid readers like me.

SARAH ALLAN DOUGLAS

Sarah Allan Douglas

I have three other great-grandparents besides John N. Walker to research in Brooklyn, but my frustration level is high. None have distinctive or unique names, so for example, when I attempt to find information on Sarah Allan (my mother's paternal grandmother), I don't know which of many Sarah Allans is mine. Ancestry.com supplied me with 1900, 1910, and 1920 U.S. Census records, and 1905, 1915, and 1925 New York State Census records. I'm confident that this is my Sarah because her husband and sons are listed at the same residence. Great-Grandpa is listed on her marriage record, death certificate, and obituary, so those are ironclad. However, any record of Sarah Allan as a young woman is anyone's guess! I was excited to find a Sarah Allan who cruised over from Ireland to the U.S. on a ship called the Germanic (built and managed by the White Star Line, same as the Titanic) in 1885. That seems about right. There's another Sarah Allan, though, who came from Ireland and disembarked in Canada. At first, I ignored that entry, believing that Brooklyn was everyone's destination, but then I found some old notes about Sarah in a notebook from my earlier attempts to decode my ancestry in the 1990s. These words were probably from my mother's mouth: "She lived in Canada and worked in a library." So, that second sailing Sarah was probably mine. Here was a connection where I could merge a remembered comment from Mom with actual evidence of a ship named the Sardinian arriving in Quebec in 1876 with an eighteen-year-old Sarah Allan on it. Is that my great-grandmother Sarah?

Information recorded by the census varies in different years. Sometimes, census takers ask about education attained, whether the subjects own or rent their home, or how long the parents have been married. In 1900, 1910, and 1920 (U.S. Census), year of immigration was asked. Sarah Allan responded, "1870" in 1900 and 1910, but "1873" in the 1920. Was the earlier date when she arrived in Canada and the later date her New York City arrival? This is better than guessing, but I'll still have to do a more detailed immigration search.

I remember my grandfather talking about his mother being a "librarian," and he had in his possession some very old, deaccessioned (withdrawn) library books. They were his treasures; he was very proud of her. I don't know what happened to those books, but I do have an autograph book that was in a box with old family photos among my mom's things. Sarah would have been my mom's grandmother, but she died when my mom was seven. I doubt my mom would have remembered her paternal grandma Sarah other than as this mythic librarian figure created by her storyteller father (my grandfather). I noticed from studying the census records that Sarah and her husband, John Harper Douglas, lived in three Brooklyn locations, ending up on 53rd Street. Did they move there because their son James Howard Douglas (known to me as Grandpa) was living on 54th Street with his young family? Maybe the grandparents were close and my mom did, in fact, know her grandmother. I still can't get used to the fact that I can't just pick up the phone to call my mom or sister. There are so many questions!

Back to the autograph book. It's brown, about four inches by two and seven-eighths, and the earliest signatures are dated 1877 when Sarah was nineteen. I don't know if an event prompted her to start keeping an autograph book (immigrating to North America?), but she continued to collect autographs until 1901. I don't have a paper trail for her before she was married in 1890. She was addressed as "Miss Allan" or, in the old-style script, "Mifs Allan" in most. Maybe someday I'll find out about a trans-Atlantic voyage, her move from Canada to New York, a graduation, or job change that inspired her to keep this remembrance. One of the autographs features this rhyme in fine, flowing fountain penmanship:

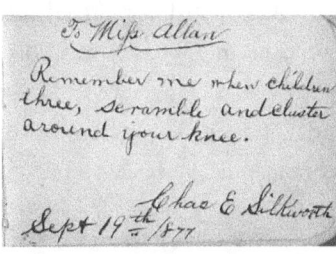

And she *did* have three children, including my Grandpa!

Sarah and John H. Douglas

Sarah Allan Douglas's husband, John Harper Douglas, has a similar genealogical record to Sarah's, living at three Brooklyn addresses after their 1890 marriage, and passing away a year after her in 1930. I know from an old copy of his citizen certificate that he became a citizen in 1880. He was born in 1853 in Bellshill, North Lanarkshire, Scotland, although the census records all state that he was born in Ireland. This discrepancy could be because the ship he sailed on to the New World emanated from Ireland, and therefore all passengers were considered Irish. About those ships: there were many men named John Douglas, as you might have guessed, but I can narrow down those choices a bit. Since I have a record that he became a citizen in 1880, he would have arrived before that. There are two ships listed, the Anglia and the Pennsylvania, with a John Douglas aboard each. I wonder if either of those could be him!

John Harper Douglas was an early participant in a unique family tradition. His initials, JHD, were carried down through four additional generations. The more recent JHDs have more distinctive names, but the earlier fellows were either John or James, adding to my genealogical difficulties. John Harper Douglas's father was James Douglas, but I don't yet have any documentation to show that he was an early JHD. Regardless, the family, especially the JHDs, takes pride in this distinctive line. It's a genealogical nomenclatural clue to our ancestors.

ARBUCKLE, PART 2: THE LAST ROAD TRIP

Fred and I took another ride up the New Jersey Turnpike, this time routed by GPS through the ultra-popular Holland Tunnel, through Lower Manhattan, and over the Brooklyn Bridge. GPS assured us that despite the delays, this was "still the fastest route." I found that hard to believe, but I was happy to go over the Brooklyn Bridge and shoot photos from the car (as a passenger). Rain had been forecasted and there were dark clouds in the sky, but as I predicted, it didn't start raining until we were at our destination.

I felt a bit of melancholy, as this was the last research trip I had planned for the *Brooklyn Family Album* project, but I was very excited to finally see the Arbuckle Sugar building where my great-grandfather, John N. Walker, worked in the 1920s and '30s. My mother used to talk about this company and his employment there, and I got the idea that she was as proud of his job as she was of her father's with the post office. I doubt she ever visited him at the Arbuckle building because he died when she was only ten - on her tenth birthday, in fact. According to his death certificate, remember, he was employed as a coffee *taster.*

We parked the car and walked down the Jay Street hill to the waterfront. According to what I've read, during its heyday, the Arbuckle company owned multiple buildings in this area where they manufactured multiple kinds of coffee under different brand names (Yuban was one of theirs) and processed sugar. The main building at 10 Jay Street had been spruced up for me (and its new corporate tenants). It's a neat, solid brick building with lots of windows on three sides. The fourth side, facing the East River, has been made to resemble sugar crystals, with glass and mirrors in a geometric design. It's really quite striking, even on a cloudy, drizzly day. On a sunny day, it must be spectacular with sunrays reflecting off those facets.

I was so excited to finally see this building that I wanted it to match the photo I have of John N. Walker with his coworkers standing in front of a garage door for a group portrait. I have to admit they are not an exact match. Both buildings are brick, but the current first-floor windows, wide enough to have been garage doors, have less of a curve to their arched tops. The old photo shows more architectural design elements worked into the brick façade that I don't think would have been feasible to remove even to satisfy modern minimalist tastes. I suppose the old photo was probably taken at a warehouse nearby. The guys are all in their shirtsleeves, some with vests, and some with suspenders, dressed for manual labor. These are not the "suits," so a warehouse would make more sense for their group portrait.

As I proclaimed to Fred multiple times as we inspected the building's exterior, I was delighted to finally see it in person. Because my mother mentioned it frequently, it felt like an authentic connection to her and her maternal grandfather. That's what I was after with this project: connections. Visceral connections. Later at home, while I looked at the photos I shot, it occurred to me I was making another cool connection. We had a baseball game on: my grand-nephew's university team was playing in the College World Series in Omaha. That young man, related to me and these ancestors, a fully-formed adult human, would be John N. Walker's great-great-great-grandson, or as they say on my favorite genealogy show, his third great-grandson. I think that's neat.

Back on the waterfront, we saw blue signs directing us to Brooklyn Bridge Park. Could this be the same park where David the photographer took our group to shoot the Brooklyn Bridge at dusk? Fred and I had come this far, fought traffic, and paid many dollars to park, so I wasn't going to let a little rain curtail my exploration. Fred was game. We followed the trail and found the exact grassy mound on which I had previously stood to take my iconic (in my head) photo, the one that now hangs giant-sized on my living room wall. The grassy mound was mere steps from the Arbuckle building. It was another Brooklyn connection, this one tying up my years-long research with a handy beginning and a convenient ending. It was a moment.

Iconic bridges had led me to Brooklyn's history, and unfamiliar sidewalks had led me to the warm comfort and awareness of genealogical details. This was the reward of my Hero's Journey, and I have, more than ever, the notion that I have sprung from that heritage. "Don't you remember me telling you about this?" I should have listened to Mom more carefully. There would be fewer mysteries and more connections similar to the types I've uncovered. After I explored Brooklyn, after I walked around downtown Brooklyn, after I examined Green-Wood Cemetery, after I skirted the perimeter of Prospect Park en route to the skating center, and after I experienced Coney Island, I finally sensed my ancestors' city.

What I am left with is a mental scrapbook of memories of my own blended with my ancestors' photographs, objects, and experiences. David the photography teacher coached us to center ourselves and our cameras in order to get that "money shot" of the Brooklyn Bridge, its pedestrian path, and its cables. My photos from his electrifying tour remind me of the beginning of the spark for my Brooklyn explorations. There's a healthy amount of informed conjecture, but more importantly, there's a well-centered *story* coming into focus.

APPENDIX 1

Here's more detail on that "Hero's Journey" concept, inspired by a great article in *Writer's Digest* (February 2014) by Elizabeth Sims:

The Hero's Journey: Basic Template

1) <u>A messenger or message appears</u>: My sister died suddenly and I was left without parents or my only sibling. I felt orphaned, and needed a new connection to family.

2) <u>A problem or challenge is presented</u>: I decided to establish some kind of connection to Brooklyn, where my mother's family lived for a few generations.

3) <u>Someone is identified as the person to solve this problem</u>: This has to be me. I don't mean to call myself a hero, but in this scenario, the hero is the person who tracks down information and makes connections.

4) <u>The challenge takes shape</u>: I will research Brooklyn by books and field trips and make connections between the present and my ancestors' city. With their WASPy Irish Protestant names, much

duplicated through the generations, my maternal ancestors are not easy to research. (Is that *my* John Walker?)

5) <u>Refusals</u>: The big one is my concern for safety, especially once COVID took shape.

6) <u>The challenge is accepted</u>: I can do this. It will take a long time. Books are easy. Research trips are harder, especially in unfamiliar territory, but I will find ways to make this work.

7) <u>The hero leaves the familiar world</u>: I planned trips to Brooklyn for various purposes, sometimes taking a taxi, and eventually conquering the subway system and subwilderment.

8) <u>Helpers materialize</u>: Amy H., Cedar Crest College cohort, Fred, Brooklyn natives, conference organizers—all contributed to this journey.

9) <u>Setbacks occur</u>: Well, soon after the challenge took shape, COVID-19 happened and I was limited to books and webinars. No excursions. Then my lung got sick with a misbehaving lymph node. I had to have the node removed, putting me on house arrest for six to eight weeks.

10) <u>The hero regroups and gains some ground</u>: I read Brooklyn-based novels and nonfiction,

conducted online research, looked for family artifacts around the house, attended webinars, and talked to people.

11) <u>The foe(s) are vanquished and the treasure is seized</u>: I made the best of the quarantine situation, eventually made some super-safe excursions, made connections between place and people, and wrote my story.

12) <u>The hero returns to the familiar world</u>: Bring on the next challenge!

Appendix 2:

Fiction About Brooklyn to set the Scene

Auster, Paul. *Sunset Park.* (Picador, 2010).

Egan, Jennifer. *Manhattan Beach.* (Scribner, 2017).

Hamill, Pete. *Snow in August.* (Little, Brown, 1997).

Jackson, Jenny. *Pineapple Street.* (Viking, 2023).

Lethem, Jonathan. *Motherless Brooklyn.* (Vintage, 1999).

McBride, James. *Deacon King Kong.* (Riverhead, 2020).

Selby, Hubert, Jr. *Last Exit to Brooklyn.* (Grove 1957).

Smith, Betty. *A Tree Grows in Brooklyn.* (Harper Perennial, 2006).

Tóibín, Colm. *Brooklyn.* (Scribner, 2009).

ABOUT THE AUTHOR

Margaret Montet is a college librarian and professor who writes and speaks about music, blending in elements of memoir, travel, art, and literature. She earned her MFA in Creative Writing from the Pan-European Program at Cedar Crest College, and a Master's in Music Theory from Temple University. In-between, she earned a Master of Library Science degree from Rutgers University. Margaret teaches Effective Speaking to college students and presents multimedia talks to community audiences around the southeastern Pennsylvania and central New Jersey region. Her creative nonfiction has been published in *The Bangalore Review*, *Clever Magazine*, *Dragon Poet Review*, *Pink Pangea*, *Flying South*, and other fine periodicals and anthologies. Her collection of travel essays, *Nerd Traveler* was released in July 2021 by Read Furiously.

Stay up to date with everything Margaret is doing at readfuriously.com/margaret-montet

A Note to our Furious Readers

From all of us at Read Furiously, we hope you enjoyed our latest installment in our One 'n Done series, *Brooklyn Family Album*.

Reading is more than a passive activity – it is the opportunity to play an active role to make our world better.

We pledge to donate a portion of these book sales to causes that are special to Read Furiously. These causes are chosen with the intent to better the lives of others who are struggling to tell their own stories.

The causes we support encourage a sense of civic responsibility associated with the act of reading. Each cause has been researched thoroughly, discussed openly, and voted upon carefully by the Read Furiously team.

To find out more about who, what, why, and where Read Furiously lends its support, please visit our website at readfuriously.com/our-causes

Happy reading and giving, Furious Readers!

Read Often, Read Well, Read Furiously!

More in the One 'n Done Series

What About Tuesday
Adam Wilson
978-0-9965227-9-3

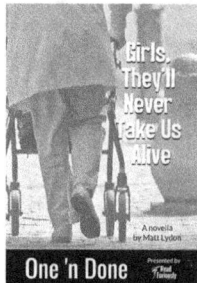

Gurls, They'll Never Take Us Alive
Matt Lydon
978-1-7337360-3-9

Brethren Hollow
Bill Hemmig
978-1-7337360-8-4

Helium
Adam Wilson
and Jeff Chin
978-1-7337360-5-3

The Legend of Dave Bradley
S Atzeni
978-1-7371758-8-9

The Path Home
A.J. Pelligrino
979-8-9868097-8-6

www.ingramcontent.com/pod-product-compliance
Lightning Source LLC
Chambersburg PA
CBHW071212120626
46546CB00006B/2525